Cheesecakes

Time-tested family favorites

PHILADELPHIA no-bake mini cheesecakes

PREP: 10 min. | TOTAL: 10 min. | MAKES: 12 servings.

▸ what you need!

1 pkg. (8 oz.) PHILADELPHIA Cream Cheese, softened

½ cup sugar

1 tub (8 oz.) COOL WHIP Whipped Topping, thawed

12 OREO Cookies

Multi-colored sprinkles

▸ make it!

BEAT cream cheese and sugar until well blended. Gently stir in COOL WHIP.

PLACE cookies on bottom of 12 paper-lined muffin cups.

SPOON cream cheese mixture into muffin cups. Top with multi-colored sprinkles. Refrigerate until ready to serve.

SUBSTITUTE:
Substitute miniature chocolate chips for sprinkles.

boston cream cheesecake

PREP: 25 min. | TOTAL: 5 hours 20 min. | MAKES: 12 servings.

▸ what you need!

1 pkg. (1-layer size) yellow cake mix

2 pkg. (8 oz. each) PHILADELPHIA Cream Cheese, softened

½ cup granulated sugar

2 tsp. vanilla, divided

2 eggs

⅓ cup BREAKSTONE'S or KNUDSEN Sour Cream

2 squares BAKER'S Unsweetened Chocolate

3 Tbsp. butter or margarine

2 Tbsp. boiling water

1 cup powdered sugar

▸ make it!

HEAT oven to 350°F.

GREASE bottom of 9-inch springform pan. Prepare cake mix as directed on package; pour batter evenly into prepared springform pan. Bake 20 min. Beat cream cheese, granulated sugar and 1 tsp. of the vanilla with electric mixer on medium speed until well blended. Add eggs, 1 at a time, mixing on low speed after each addition just until blended. Blend in sour cream; pour over cake layer.

BAKE an additional 35 min. or until center is almost set. Run knife or metal spatula around rim of pan to loosen cake; cool before removing rim of pan.

MELT chocolate and butter in medium saucepan over low heat, stirring until smooth. Remove from heat. Add water, powdered sugar and remaining 1 tsp. vanilla; mix well. Spread over cooled cheesecake. Refrigerate 4 hours or overnight.

cappuccino cheesecake

PREP: 25 min. | TOTAL: 6 hours 35 min. | MAKES: 16 servings.

▸ what you need!

1½ cups finely chopped PLANTERS Walnuts

3 Tbsp. butter or margarine, melted

2 Tbsp. sugar

4 pkg. (8 oz. each) PHILADELPHIA Cream Cheese, softened

1 cup sugar

3 Tbsp. flour

4 eggs

1 cup BREAKSTONE'S or KNUDSEN Sour Cream

1 Tbsp. MAXWELL HOUSE Instant Coffee

¼ tsp. ground cinnamon

¼ cup boiling water

1½ cups thawed COOL WHIP Whipped Topping

▸ make it!

HEAT oven to 325°F.

MIX nuts, butter and 2 Tbsp. sugar; press onto bottom of 9-inch springform pan. Bake 10 min. Remove from oven; cool. Increase oven temperature to 450°F.

BEAT cream cheese, 1 cup sugar and flour with mixer until well blended. Add eggs, 1 at a time, mixing on low speed after each just until blended. Blend in sour cream.

DISSOLVE instant coffee with cinnamon in water; cool. Gradually add to cream chees mixture, mixing until well blended. Pour over crust.

BAKE 10 min. Reduce oven temperature to 250°F. Bake an additional 1 hour or until center is almost set. Run knife around rim of pan to loosen cake; cool before removing rim. Refrigerate 4 hours. Top with dollops of COOL WHIP. Garnish with a sprinkle of additional cinnamon, if desired.

NOTE:
Reduce oven temperature to 300°F if using a dark nonstick springform pan.

white chocolate-cranberry cheesecake

PREP: 15 min. | **TOTAL:** 5 hours 5 min. | **MAKES:** 12 servings.

▸ what you need!

15 OREO Cookies, finely crushed (about 1¼ cups)

¼ cup butter, melted

3 pkg. (8 oz. each) PHILADELPHIA Cream Cheese, softened

¾ cup sugar

3 eggs

4 squares BAKER'S White Chocolate, melted

½ cup dried cranberries

1 tsp. grated orange zest

▸ make it!

HEAT oven to 350°F.

MIX cookie crumbs and butter. Press firmly onto bottom of 9-inch springform pan.

BEAT cream cheese and sugar in large bowl with electric mixer on medium speed until well blended. Add eggs, 1 at a time, mixing just until blended after each addition. Stir in white chocolate, cranberries and orange zest; pour over crust.

BAKE 45 to 50 min. or until center is almost set if using a silver springform pan. (Or, bake at 325°F for 45 to 50 min. if using a dark nonstick springform pan.) Cool completely. Refrigerate 3 hours or overnight.

SPECIAL EXTRA:
Garnish with thawed COOL WHIP Whipped Topping, orange slices and additional dried cranberries just before serving.

chocolate-hazelnut cheesecake

PREP: 30 min. | TOTAL: 5 hours 35 min. | MAKES: 16 servings.

what you need!

18 OREO Cookies, crushed (about 1½ cups)

2 Tbsp. butter or margarine, melted

3 pkg. (8 oz. each) PHILADELPHIA Cream Cheese, softened

1 cup sugar

1 tsp. vanilla

1 pkg. (8 squares) BAKER'S Semi-Sweet Chocolate, melted, slightly cooled

¼ cup hazelnut-flavored liqueur

3 eggs

½ cup whole hazelnuts, toasted

make it!

HEAT oven to 325°F if using a silver 9-inch springform pan (or to 300°F if using a dark nonstick 9-inch springform pan).

MIX crushed cookies and butter; press firmly onto bottom of pan. Bake 10 min.

BEAT cream cheese, sugar and vanilla in large bowl with electric mixer on medium speed until well blended. Add chocolate and liqueur; mix well. Add eggs, 1 at a time, mixing on low speed after each addition just until blended. Pour over crust.

BAKE 55 min. to 1 hour 5 min. or until center is almost set. Run knife or metal spatula around rim of pan to loosen cake; cool before removing rim of pan. Refrigerate 4 hours or overnight. Top with nuts just before serving.

PHILADELPHIA new york-style strawberry swirl cheesecake

PREP: 15 min. | TOTAL: 5 hours 25 min. | MAKES: 16 servings.

▸ what you need!

1 cup HONEY MAID Graham Cracker Crumbs

3 Tbsp. sugar

3 Tbsp. butter, melted

5 pkg. (8 oz. each) PHILADELPHIA Cream Cheese, softened

1 cup sugar

3 Tbsp. flour

1 Tbsp. vanilla

1 cup BREAKSTONE'S or KNUDSEN Sour Cream

4 eggs

⅓ cup seedless strawberry jam

▸ make it!

HEAT oven to 325°F.

LINE 13×9-inch pan with foil, with ends of foil extending over sides. Mix graham crumbs, 3 Tbsp. sugar and butter; press onto bottom of pan. Bake 10 min.

BEAT cream cheese, 1 cup sugar, flour and vanilla in large bowl with mixer until well blended. Add sour cream; mix well. Add eggs, 1 at a time, mixing on low speed after each just until blended. Pour over crust. Gently drop small spoonfuls of jam over batter; swirl with knife.

BAKE 40 min. or until center is almost set. Cool completely. Refrigerate 4 hours. Lift cheesecake from pan with foil handles before cutting to serve.

double-decker OREO cheesecake

PREP: 25 min. | TOTAL: 5 hours 40 min. | MAKES: 16 servings.

▸ what you need!

1 pkg. (1 lb. 1 oz.) OREO Chocolate Creme Cookies (48 cookies), divided

¼ cup butter, melted

4 pkg. (8 oz. each) PHILADELPHIA Cream Cheese, softened

1 cup sugar

1 tsp. vanilla

1 cup BREAKSTONE'S or KNUDSEN Sour Cream

4 eggs

4 squares BAKER'S Semi-Sweet Chocolate, melted

▸ make it!

HEAT oven to 325°F.

PROCESS 30 cookies in food processor until finely ground. Add butter; mix well. Press onto bottom of 13×9-inch baking pan.

BEAT cream cheese, sugar and vanilla in large bowl with mixer until well blended. Add sour cream; mix well. Add eggs, 1 at a time, beating after each just until blended; pour half over crust. Stir melted chocolate into remaining batter; pour over batter in pan. Chop remaining cookies; sprinkle over batter.

BAKE 45 min. or until center is almost set. Cool completely. Refrigerate 4 hours.

SIZE-WISE:
Enjoy your favorite foods while keeping portion size in mind.

MAKE AHEAD:
Wrap cooled cheesecake tightly in foil. Freeze up to 2 months. Thaw in refrigerator overnight before serving.

HOW TO REMOVE FROM PAN EASILY:
Line pan with foil, with ends of foil extending over sides. Prepare as directed. Use foil handles to lift cheesecake from pan before cutting.

white chocolate-cherry pecan cheesecake

PREP: 30 min. | TOTAL: 6 hours 30 min. | MAKES: 16 servings.

▸ what you need!

- 1 cup PLANTERS Pecan Halves, toasted, divided
- 1½ cups HONEY MAID Graham Cracker Crumbs
- ¼ cup sugar
- ¼ cup margarine or butter, melted
- 3 pkg. (8 oz. each) PHILADELPHIA Cream Cheese, softened
- 1 can (14 oz.) sweetened condensed milk
- 1 pkg. (6 squares) BAKER'S White Chocolate, melted
- 2 tsp. vanilla, divided
- 4 eggs
- 1 can (21 oz.) cherry pie filling
- 1 cup thawed COOL WHIP Whipped Topping

▸ make it!

HEAT oven to 300°F if using a silver 9-inch springform pan (or to 275°F if using a dark nonstick 9-inch springform pan).

RESERVE 16 nut halves. Finely chop remaining nuts; mix with graham crumbs, sugar and margarine. Press firmly onto bottom of pan.

BEAT cream cheese in large bowl with electric mixer on medium speed until creamy. Gradually add sweetened condensed milk, beating until well blended. Add chocolate and 1 tsp. of the vanilla; mix well. Add eggs, 1 at a time, mixing on low speed just until blended. Pour over crust.

BAKE 1 hour or until center is almost set. Run knife around rim of pan to loosen cake; cool before removing rim. Refrigerate 4 hours or overnight.

MIX pie filling and remaining vanilla; spoon over cheesecake. Top with COOL WHIP and reserved nut halves.

NILLA praline cheesecake

PREP: 20 min. | TOTAL: 6 hours 5 min. | MAKES: 16 servings.

▸ what you need!

66 NILLA Wafers, divided

1¼ cups sugar, divided

¼ cup margarine or butter, melted

3 pkg. (8 oz. each) PHILADELPHIA Cream Cheese, softened

½ cup BREAKSTONE'S or KNUDSEN Sour Cream

1 tsp. vanilla

3 eggs

25 KRAFT Caramels

3 Tbsp. milk

½ cup PLANTERS Pecan Pieces, toasted

▸ make it!

HEAT oven to 325°F.

FINELY crush 50 wafers; mix with ¼ cup sugar and margarine. Press onto bottom of 9-inch springform pan. Stand remaining wafers around edge, pressing gently into crust to secure.

BEAT cream cheese and remaining sugar in large bowl with mixer until well blended. Add sour cream and vanilla; mix well. Add eggs, 1 at a time, beating on low speed after each just until blended. Pour over crust.

BAKE 45 to 50 min. or until center is almost set. Run small knife around rim of pan to loosen cake; cool before removing rim. Refrigerate 4 hours. Microwave caramels and milk on HIGH 1 min. or until caramels are completely melted, stirring every 30 sec. Cool slightly. Pour over cheesecake; top with nuts.

SUBSTITUTE:
Line 13×9-inch pan with foil, with ends of foil extending over sides. Grease foil. Prepare recipe as directed, increasing whole NILLA Wafers around the side from 16 to 22. Bake 40 to 45 min. or until center is almost set. Use foil handles to lift dessert from pan before cutting into squares to serve.

NOTE:
If using a dark nonstick 9-inch springform pan, reduce oven temperature to 300°F.

HOW TO TOAST NUTS:
Toasting nuts adds crunch and intensifies their flavor. To toast nuts in the oven, spread nuts in single layer in shallow baking pan. Bake at 350°F for 10 to 15 min. or until golden brown, stirring occasionally.

OREO no-bake cheesecake

PREP: 15 min. | **TOTAL:** 4 hours 15 min. | **MAKES:** 16 servings, 1 piece each.

▸ what you need!

1 pkg. (16.6 oz.) OREO Cookies, divided

¼ cup butter, melted

4 pkg. (8 oz. each) PHILADELPHIA Cream Cheese, softened

½ cup sugar

1 tsp. vanilla

1 tub (8 oz.) COOL WHIP Whipped Topping, thawed

▸ make it!

LINE 13×9-inch pan with foil, with ends of foil extending over sides of pan. Coarsely chop 15 of the cookies; set aside. Finely crush remaining cookies; mix with butter. Press firmly onto bottom of prepared pan. Refrigerate while preparing filling.

BEAT cream cheese, sugar and vanilla in large bowl with electric mixer on medium speed until well blended. Gently stir in COOL WHIP and chopped cookies. Spoon over crust; cover.

REFRIGERATE 4 hours or until firm. Store leftover cheesecake in refrigerator.

VARIATION:
Prepare as directed, using 1 pkg. (1 lb. 2 oz.) Golden OREO Cookies or 1 pkg. (1 lb. 1 oz.) OREO Cool Mint Creme Cookies.

chocolate-berry no-bake cheesecake

PREP: 15 min. | TOTAL: 3 hours 15 min. | MAKES: 10 servings.

▸ what you need!

2 squares BAKER'S Semi-Sweet Chocolate

2 pkg. (8 oz. each) PHILADELPHIA Cream Cheese, softened

⅓ cup sugar

2 cups thawed COOL WHIP Chocolate Whipped Topping

1 OREO Pie Crust (6 oz.)

1½ cups quartered strawberries

▸ make it!

MICROWAVE chocolate in small microwaveable bowl on HIGH 1 min.; stir until chocolate is completely melted. Set aside.

BEAT cream cheese and sugar in large bowl with electric mixer on medium speed until well blended. Add chocolate, mix well. Gently stir in COOL WHIP. Spoon into crust.

REFRIGERATE 3 hours or until set. Top with strawberries just before serving. Store leftover cheesecake in refrigerator.

PHILADELPHIA blueberry no-bake cheesecake

PREP: 15 min. | TOTAL: 4 hours 15 min. | MAKES: 16 servings.

▸ what you need!

2 cups HONEY MAID Graham Cracker Crumbs

6 Tbsp. margarine, melted

1 cup sugar, divided

4 pkg. (8 oz. each) PHILADELPHIA Neufchâtel Cheese, softened

½ cup blueberry preserves

Grated zest from 1 lemon

1 pkg. (16 oz.) frozen blueberries, thawed, drained

1 tub (8 oz.) COOL WHIP LITE Whipped Topping, thawed

▸ make it!

MIX graham crumbs, margarine and ¼ cup of the sugar; press firmly onto bottom of 13×9-inch pan. Refrigerate while preparing filling.

BEAT Neufchâtel cheese and remaining ¾ cup sugar in large bowl with electric mixer on medium speed until well blended. Add preserves and lemon zest, mix until blended. Stir in blueberries. Gently stir in COOL WHIP. Spoon over crust; cover.

REFRIGERATE 4 hours or until firm. Garnish as desired. Store leftovers in refrigerator.

HOW TO MAKE IT WITH FRESH BLUEBERRIES:
Place 2 cups blueberries in small bowl with 2 Tbsp. sugar; mash with fork. Add to Neufchâtel cheese mixture; continue as directed.

PHILADELPHIA classic cheesecake

PREP: 20 min. | TOTAL: 5 hours 45 min. | MAKES: 16 servings.

▸ what you need!

1½ cups HONEY MAID Graham Cracker Crumbs

3 Tbsp. sugar

⅓ cup butter or margarine, melted

4 pkg. (8 oz. each) PHILADELPHIA Cream Cheese, softened

1 cup sugar

1 tsp. vanilla

4 eggs

▸ make it!

HEAT oven to 325°F.

MIX graham crumbs, 3 Tbsp. sugar and butter; press onto bottom of 9-inch springform pan.

BEAT cream cheese, 1 cup sugar and vanilla with mixer until well blended. Add eggs, 1 at a time, mixing on low speed after each just until blended. Pour over crust.

BAKE 55 min. or until center is almost set. Loosen cake from rim of pan; cool before removing rim. Refrigerate 4 hours.

SIZE-WISE:
Sweets can add enjoyment to a balanced diet, but remember to keep tabs on portions.

SPECIAL EXTRA:
Top with fresh fruit just before serving.